John,

To paraph[ra]... ...ott

" he best way to be a

millionaire as a music

6 Keys

promoter...

to Success

How to Run a Band

Be Famous &

Change the World

Dan Van Casteele

... start with two millon!"

6 Keys

to Success

How to Run a Band

Be Famous &

Change the World

Dan Van Casteele

Published by 22 Lions Bookstore

www.22Lions.com

Table of Contents

About

About the Bookstore:

www.22Lions.com

Facebook.com/22Lions

Twitter.com/22lionsbookshop

Instagram.com/22lionsbookshop

Pinterest.com/22lionsbookshop

Introduction

Even though most people think that fame depends on luck, the best bands follow a completely different mindset and route by shaping their fate. Their rules are so common that anyone with enough success and experience will easily identity them. And yet, they're also completely hidden from a majority in the music industry that can't see it.

This book will reveal to you what only famous bands know. These are secrets that will allow you to reach popularity and a great reputation much faster and with more impact, not just locally, but worldwide.

Maybe you're creating your own band, trying to reinvent the one you have, or simply searching for ways to take what you have one step further into the fame it deserves. Whatever is the situation, this book will guide you there.

The main rules for success are here explained with a direct and simple vocabulary, allowing you to easily correlate the information to any band you know and see that, more than a theory, this book refers to very obvious facts that can be identified and measured.

1. Choose a Niche

Choosing your music niche doesn't have to be something that you do on purpose. It can simply be just something that you find. Who enjoys your music? Who goes to your parties? Maybe the answer to these questions isn't necessarily the one you want to hear but you have to really think about it. Because, either you change your style, or you appeal to your dedicated audience.

Generally speaking, people know your worth and will react accordingly, telling you exactly where and how you should play to be more successful. Many of today's famous bands started in very small niches and expanded from there. But you do need to have your roots well rooted and that's the ground of your first audience.

You may realize the answer to those questions by observing how your audience uses your music and for which ends they use it. Maybe your style is more suitable for those interested in radical sports, underground environments, aggressive environments, or merely for individual appreciation. Either way, you always have a target.

People that enjoy listening to your music while alone are also a specific niche in the market, and the band may start failing in its goals if it tries to transform such individuals into a crowd.

On the other hand, the success of your band may take longer to occur that expected, especially if you're not involved exclusively in targeting your audience but trying to reach as many niches as possible. The greed for success has become the ending point where many bands fail and depart.

Play close attention to your followers and allow them to use your music to create their own videos. In this way, you'll get a faster access to how they see you. Notice the feelings in the videos, the words they use and how they are used, and then find a way to match that with your nature.

The most popular bands eventually satisfy their audience while maximizing their creativity, and they do it by tapping into what they love the most about their followers.

2. Have a Good Message

Nobody truly wants to know the meaning of the lyrics in a song or video. But humans are fundamentally emotional beings. In other words, a song becomes more relevant and meaningful when related to how they feel about themselves and life in general.

The connection that music allows can reach other goals as well. For exemple, you can make your listeners feel more connected with their emotions and dream more easily.

Music can be motivating, inspiring, empowering and, most of all, the best companion. When you can make a song become personal to millions, that's when you become really successful. This is the reason why some bands, even though seemingly not making any sense with their lyrics, or misinterpreting symbols and meanings, can still be a success.

However, I'm not saying that the lyrics aren't important. They do have meaning and purpose, and they do influence emotions and behaviors, but it is how the words are communicated and in which emotions they communicate that matters the most.

Many modern singers and bands have found ways to compensate what they couldn't do with their lyrics. Performances in live concerts are one example. The other, not less important, are videoclips. But videos must tell stories, and they should be as realistic or as related to reality as possible. The music video must not only tell a story but also make the audience feel that it's their story. If people can relate to your story, and feel identified with the lyrics, then they will surely even redefine themselves with the band members, and seek everything about them as if they were family members.

Dramatization and exaggeration may not be well received by the media or even certain segments of society, but you must be raw if you want to be honest, and the courage to be honest is highly appreciated by those that like to listen to bands. It is as if the band was speaking with them, for them and specially what they can't or wish they could.

If you can motivate and inspire, then the level you are reaching is even higher than what you will reach with merely special effects and the rights words.

If you lack inspiration, look at our history and the news on tv, and you will find your way. Know also the problems of your followers, by directly speaking with them and listening to them, and in the end you will know what they want to hear. And that means being inspiring as a band. That's what cool bands do.

The more real-life stories you can tell, the better, even if you have to tell the story of a particular person rejected and not listened by society. Usually, such stories are related to human values and dreams. But you can also take your creativity one step further, and use speeches and interviews, even if you have to create them yourself. Don't wait for the movie industry to take your music and bring a movie to your songs instead.

3. Evolve and Improve

Bands are not equal among themselves. There are levels and steps that must be known.

Usually the members of a band want to copy their idols. And that's okay. But it's not enough. First, you naturally learn about your favorite songs. Then you combine the best tricks, sequences and ideas that you know. From these ideas, you can create a specific goal, within which you form your own style. Nothing is really new in music anyway, but bands do upgrade their musical quality by reinventing it with what is available.

If you pay attention and do your own research, you'll easily notice how fast music has evolved in the past years by following these principles. Great bands are always reinventing what already exists and pulling it higher to a new level of experience.

Nonetheless, you may have to choose your fans as well. What kind of people do you want to have around you? What are they into and what do they expect? In the end, it's all about reaching a perfect equilibrium between your qualities, the expectations others have and what is new in your sound.

As time goes by, you will definitely have to perfect yourself as any other band would. Look at old bands like Metallica, Megadeth, The Prodigy, and so many others out there, and you will see that their sound has become more clean, simple and precise over the years. They have also found and eliminated their weak points, while focusing on the strong ones. And, yes, sometimes this may include adding new members or letting others go. It all depends on how successful you want to be and how fast you want it.

The ultimately level is reached when the band has no ego anymore or even the personalization of ideas. And this means investing on the success of the band with commitment and beyond personal quarrels and prejudices. It also means sacrificing your personal life, including your love life.

The band, at this last point, is a living organism, and the members are nothing more than its cells. They will feel and live merely through the band. The heart of the band will beat as one, and there are no guitars, fans or music anymore but just a constant and common exploration of new realities.

Great bands spend more time on the road, doing concerts, finding opportunities for concerts, failing, learning from the failures, and moving on as if nothing bad had happened, instead of creating new music. And I'm not saying that creating new tracks isn't important, but that it's just one part, one small piece of the whole picture you are trying to manifest.

4. Know Your Weaknesses

An album is composed of music, so you must divide its songs. Then, you must look at each song as having different parts, and divide them as well. After that, allow the fans to tell you which ones are the best songs, which part of each song is the best part, and search for a balance by abandoning the weaknesses found.

In order to reach your highest potential, you must set pride aside. It consists in being realistic and accepting facts without criticism or self-judgment, as we are often wrongly used to do and therefore conditioning our mind in the wrong way. As an example, if the singer is the soul of the band, she's the one that will allow the fans to feel gratified and happy. She'll also be the one that will bring people to the concerts. This fact mustn't be neglected and must be indeed explored. You can learn from similar personalities which traits are the best when adding more attributes.

If there is a member in the band that is like a tower, confident and aggressive, we can explore this factor with the audience, as he can use it to excite them. In other words, you must enhance what you look like and what is appreciated as well. And maybe this is difficult in the beginning but, as times goes by, you may even like it and feel more capable, just as in any acting job. Maybe this person has just, simply putting it, not shout enough during his lifetime.

This said, never forget the drum-player. He is, in many aspects, the soul of the band. And he must be sensitive enough to detect the right speed in which he must be playing, as well as the unpredictable moments, in which the speed slightly changes, adulterating everything that he has learned about music.

Rules are very important when creating music but are the least important thing when you need to reinvent it.

5. Create an Ideal Balance

Some members in a band are more emotional and others are more physical or mental. In other words, some people like to feel more, others prefer to express more, and still for others music is a mental experience, a path to alternative realities. And, as a band, you most know how to coordinate all these assets as if it was one single being trying to live with himself.

When these factors are well-coordinated, the rest, including unexpected mistakes, become far less important. If the members of the band can, at least, be conscious of this, half of the work has been done already.

I don't know if you like the Spice Girls but the fact is that they're one of the fastest selling bands and they have applied these principles very well, allowing themselves to come from a place where they were not even known to a massive success in a short period of time. All the fans of the Spice Girls, can, at least, identify with one of them. And even if you don't like their music, I'm sure you have memorized at least one of their stage names.

The personalization, or building of the character of a band, demands four things: a conscious awareness of the clothes that are being used, the alterego of each element, the face of the band and the leadership of the band.

Starting with the clothes, I again refer the Prodigy and Metallica as being among the best examples. They can be original, simple, casual and inspiring at the same time. But specific niches like the Cybergoth movement, the Gothics and the followers of EBM are able to achieve the same thing quite well and exemplary.

I personally don't think that it's a good idea for each member of the band to dress as he wants, even though distinctions must be clear enough. In the end, there should be a certain harmony and clearly identifiable fashion element in the band.

As bands move up the scale of popularity, they all eventually realize this. You simply need to observe how certain famous bands look now and how they looked when doing their first interviews. The contrast is too obvious to be ignored.

The elements of the band should also be dressed according to what they play, because the image of the band is as important as the music, and both must be synchronized. The band doesn't need to sell its soul to success, but it does need to learn to be professional in order to reach success. And being professional means realizing that playing music is a job of management and marketing, in which image is, and sorry to say it, extremely important.

6. Act Professionally

Do not copy the past but get inspired in it to recreate a new future. Be part of a band you would like to have seen, not the one you saw! Find the right combination of colors and use them not only in the clothes, but the instruments as well, the lights in your show, and so on.

In the end, whatever you do, never forget that you are part of a band wherever you go and whatever you do, even when you do interviews or take pictures. It will always affect the image of the whole group for better or worse.

If you want to be a professional musician, you must act like one, by respecting your agreements and commitments, speaking properly and respectfully, and always arriving on time.

Who you are isn't important. What you do is.

When people proudly tell me that they're members of a band, I know immediately that they can't be very good. Because good musicians don't present themselves, they present their work instead. They don't say: "I'm the member of a band". They say : "listen to this and let me know your thoughts".

They aren't necessarily searching for criticism when doing this and asking such questions, but merely trying to find ways to promote themselves and improve their work. Bands with potential for success always look beyond what the eyes can see and search for ideas hidden behind comments.

Before knowing what it is to be famous, you must, at least, think already like a famous person. That has nothing to do with arrogance, but everything to do with knowing how to be honest and responsible.

Booklist

1. 6 Keys to Success

2. Anyone Can DJ

3. The Portuguese Music

4. The Path to Success

Bookstore

This book was published by the 22 Lions Bookstore.

For more books visit www.22Lions.com.

Printed in Great Britain
by Amazon

10632157R00020